MINISTRY OF MUNITIONS.

Technical Department—Aircraft Production.

I.O. 636.

KINGSWAY,
W.C. 2

REPORT ON THE

PFALZ

SINGLE-SEATER.

JULY, 1918.

The Naval & Military Press Ltd

Published by
The Naval & Military Press Ltd
5 Riverside, Brambleside, Bellbrook
Industrial Estate, Uckfield, East Sussex,
TN22 1QQ England

Tel: +44 (0) 1825 749494
Fax: +44 (0) 1825 765701

www.naval-military-press.com
www.military-genealogy.com

In reprinting in facsimile from the original, any imperfections are inevitably reproduced and the quality may fall short of modern type and cartographic standards.

MINISTRY OF MUNITIONS.

Technical Department—Aircraft Production.

I.O. 636.

KINGSWAY,
W.C. 2

REPORT ON THE
PFALZ
SINGLE-SEATER.

JULY, 1918.

REPORT

ON

The Pfalz Single-Seater (G.141.)

This machine landed in the British lines near Bonnieul on the 26th February, 1918. It is a single-seater scout of interesting design. The number D.3, 4184/17 is painted on the fuselage. From its light construction and clean design, and from the great amount of care that has been taken to keep the fuselage of very good stream-line shape and so free from irregularities, it appears to be the result of a serious attempt to produce a scout machine with good performance.

In this connection the actual performance of the aeroplane as given below is especially interesting and instructive.

Some leading particulars follow:—

Weight empty	1,532 lbs.
Total weight	2,056 lbs.
Area of upper wings	151.6 sq. ft.
Area of lower wings	88.4 sq. ft.
Total area of wings	240 sq. ft.
Loading per sq. ft. of wing surface	8.56 lbs.
Area of aileron, each	10.25 sq. ft.
Area of balance of aileron	.6 sq. ft.
Area of tail plane	12.1 sq. ft.
Area of fin	2.8 sq. ft.
Area of rudder	6.0 sq. ft.
Area of elevators	12.7 sq. ft.
Total weight per H.P.	12.84 lbs.
Crew	1
Armament	2 Spandau guns firing through propeller
Engine	160 H.P. Mercedes
Petrol capacity	21½ gallons
Oil capacity	4 gallons

PERFORMANCE.

(a) Climb to 5,000 ft.	6 min. 55 sec.
Rate of climb in ft. per min.	605
Indicated air speed	73 m.p.h.
Revolutions of engine	1,330
(b) Climb to 10,000 ft.	17 min. 30 sec.
Rate of climb in ft. per min.	360
Indicated air speed	67 m.p.h.
Revolutions of engine	1,310
(c) Climb to 15,000 ft.	41 min. 20 sec.
Rate of climb in ft. per min.	110
Indicated air speed	50 m.p.h.
Revolutions of engine	1280

SPEED.

At 10,000 ft.	102½ m.p.h.
At 15,000 ft.	91½ m.p.h.
Service ceiling at which rate of climb is 100 ft. per min.	15,800
Estimated absolute ceiling	17,000
Greatest height reached	15,000 ft.
Rate of climb at this height	110 ft. per min.
Air endurance	About 2½ hours
Military load	281 lbs.

STABILITY AND MANŒUVREABILITY.

This machine is reported to be stable laterally and unstable directionally and longitudinally. It answers well to all controls, much better than does the Albatros D.5, but tends to turn to the left in flight. It is not tiring to fly, and is normally easy to land. Though the tail skid is of the non-steering type, no difficulty is found in directing the machine on the ground.

VIEW.

As may be expected from the shape and disposition of the wings, the view is excellent in all directions—except, perhaps, on a downward glide, when the top plane interferes to some extent.

WINGS.

The wings and wing bracing are a copy of Nieuport practice. The top plane is in one piece, and has no dihedral angle. The smaller lower planes have a dihedral angle of 1 deg.

In flying position the leading edge of the upper plane is 15 inches in front of the leading edge of the lower plane.

Ailerons are fitted to the upper wings only, and both upper and lower planes have the characteristic wash-out at the tips.

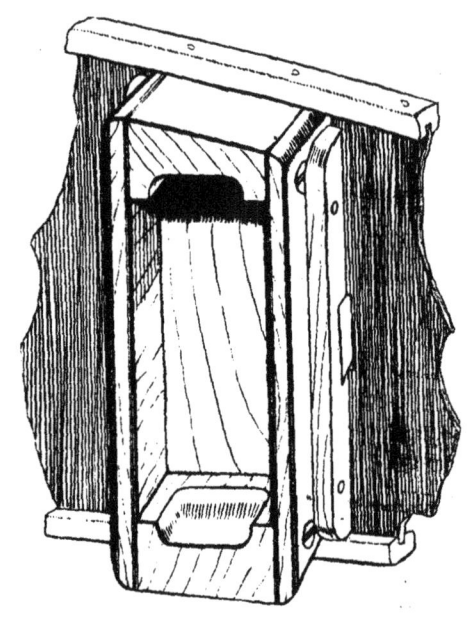

Fig. 1.

WING CONSTRUCTION.

The spars of this machine are well worthy of attention. The webs are made of a thick central core of good straight grained wood, covered on each side with one layer of extremely thin 3-ply. The 3-ply stiffens up the webs against buckling inwards, thus enabling thinner webs to be used than if not reinforced. The flanges are spindled to give

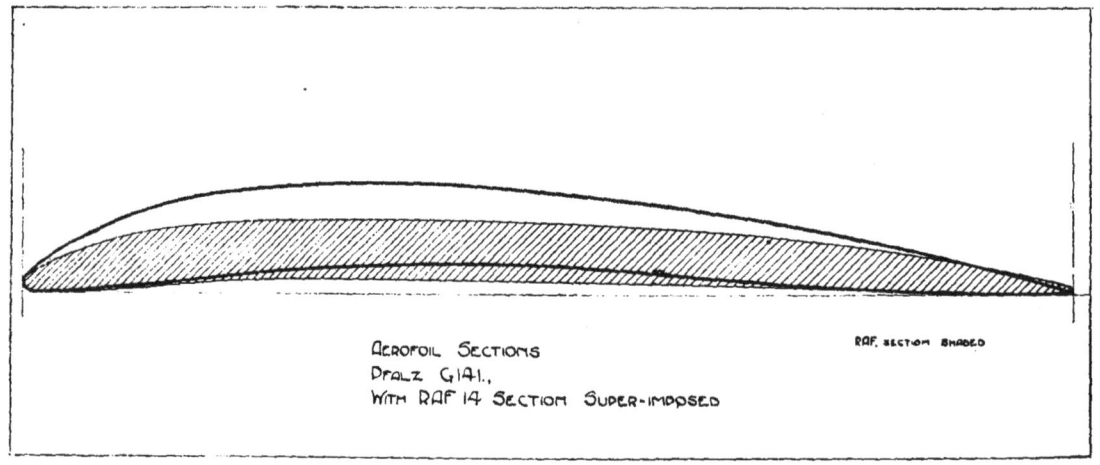

Fig. 2.

good glueing area and fillet, and diaphragms are fixed at each rib to transmit the shear stress across the spar. This is a good feature, and might with advantage be incorporated in all box spars.

These several points are clearly shown in Fig. 1.

The ribs are built up in the usual way of 3-ply and flanges, and are of light construction. The wing section, with R.A.F. 14 Section superimposed for purposes of comparison, appears in Fig. 2, and Fig. 3 gives an idea of the rib construction.

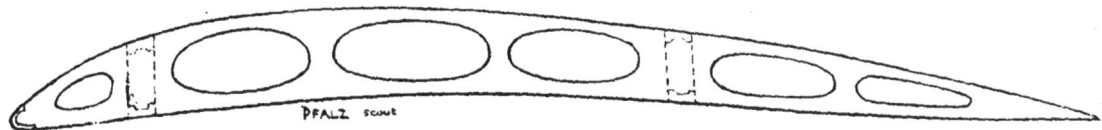

Fig. 3.

They are placed 350 mm. apart, and auxiliary ribs are placed alternately with the true ribs. The internal bracing presents no novel feature, the usual steel compression tubes being braced with piano wire and swaged rod.

The ailerons are balanced, the area of the balanced portion being .6 sq. ft. They work in the usual way with the aileron lever passing through a slot in the upper plane.

STRUTS.

As there is no dihedral angle to the upper plane, the usual cabane type of centre section is not found. Instead, the centre section struts slope outwards, as can be seen in the photographs.

The lower extremity of the V strut is not a point, but each separate limb of the Vee is fixed to a steel tube incorporated in the wing structure. This is made quite clear in Fig. 4. The struts themselves are built up solidly of wood.

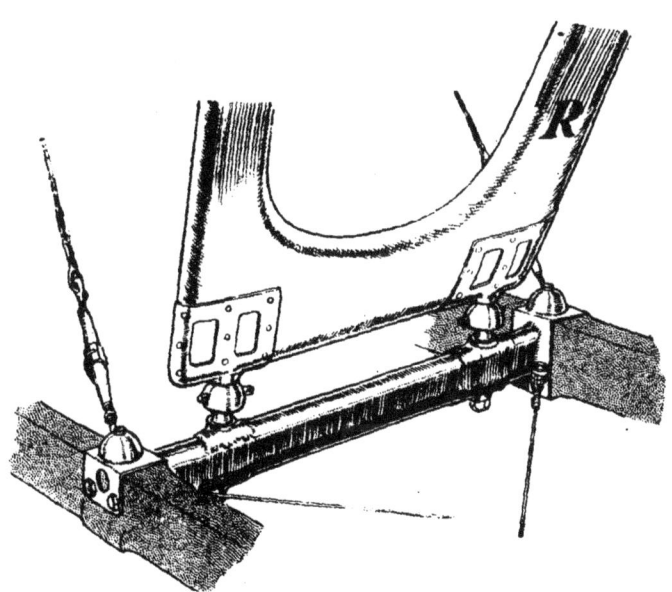

Fig. 4.

FUSELAGE.

This is by far the most novel feature of the Pfalz. The fuselage is simply a light wooden framework, without any bracing, covered with two skins of three-ply. These skins are arranged spirally in different directions. This construction, as well as the method of splicing the three-ply is shown in Figs. 5 and 6. This lends itself to the very characteristic way in which the lower wings are faired off into the fuselage. The fuselage section is oval

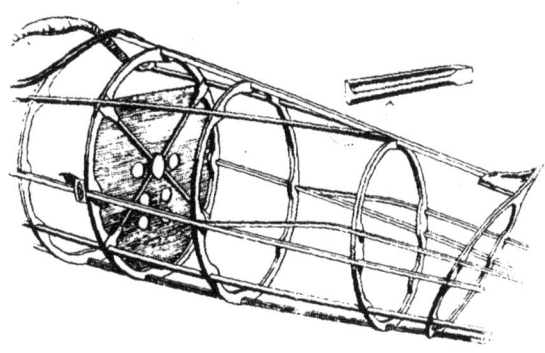

Fig. 5.

throughout its whole length. It is obviously of excellent stream-line shape, but pilots have reported a tendency to whip when machine is in flight. Only the nose and engine cowl are of aluminium.

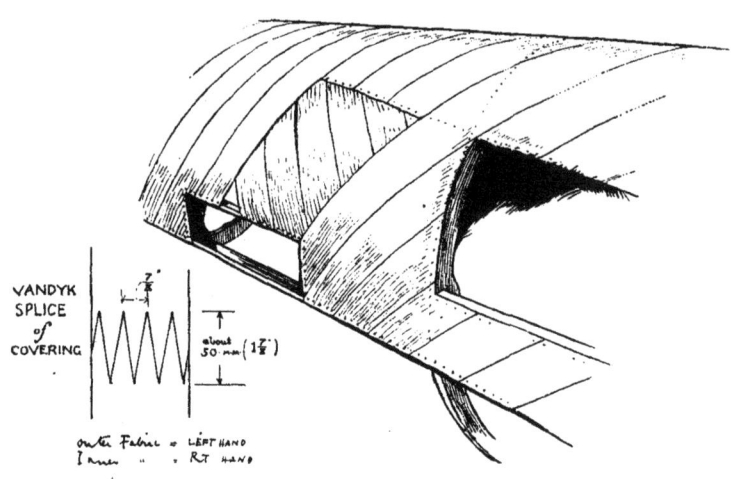

Fig. 6.

A good idea of the appearance of the fore-part of the fuselage, as well as of the way in which the lower plane merges by means of a rather elaborate three-ply fairing into the body, is given by Fig. 7, and by the various photographs of the aeroplane.

Another view of this feature—the junction of lower plane and fuselage—is presented in Fig. 9. Both of these sketches also serve to show the large number of aluminium traps or doors with which the front part of the body is provided. These doors all have some locking device, designed to give a minimum of trouble to operate, which guarantees the shut position of the doors during flight.

Fig. 7.

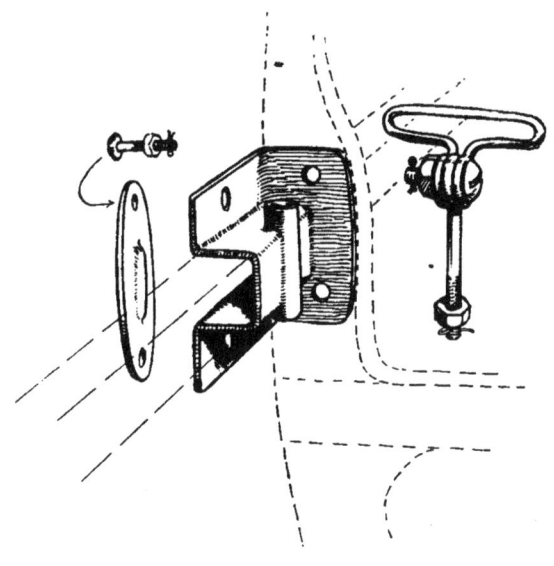

Fig. 8.

This shows the safety-belt anchorage, which incidentally serves as a strengthening for the fuselage framework.

UNDERCARRIAGE.

This is of the usual Vee type, and is constructed of stream-lined steel tube. Both the front and rear limbs are of similar section, the greater diameter being 48 mm. and the lesser 31 mm. No wooden fairing is fitted. The axle lies between the two wooden compression struts, and is covered by an aluminium lid, hinged at the front side, which is kept in place by the pressure of the air. The shock absorbers are of rubber, which is somewhat unusual in German aeroplanes at present.

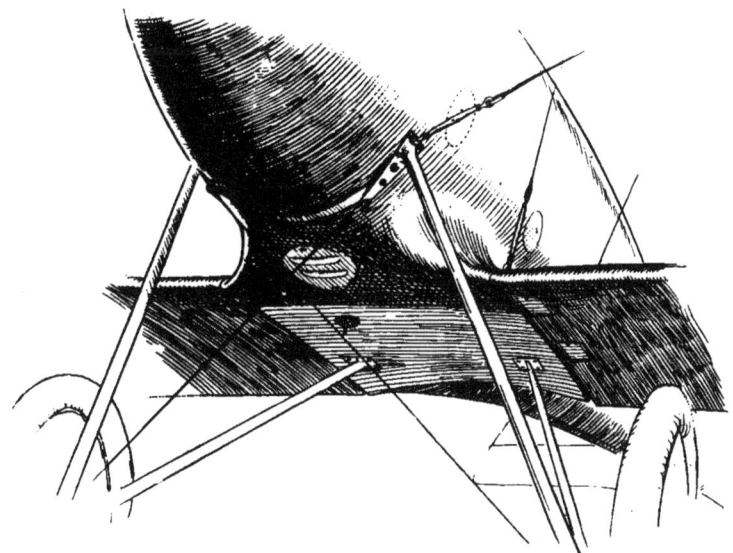

Fig. 9.

CONTROLS.

The control lever works a longitudinal rocking shaft, which in turn actuates the ailerons. The aileron cables pass through the wings, and are covered with a varnished tube very neatly made of rolled paper. The elevators are worked by cables taken direct from the control lever—one above and one below the pivot. The elevator controls can be quickly locked by the simple device shown in Fig. 11.

THE RUDDER BAR.

This is, as usual, of welded sheet steel, but is capable of some adjustment, as may be seen on reference to Fig. 10. All control cables lie for the greater part of their length within the fuselage.

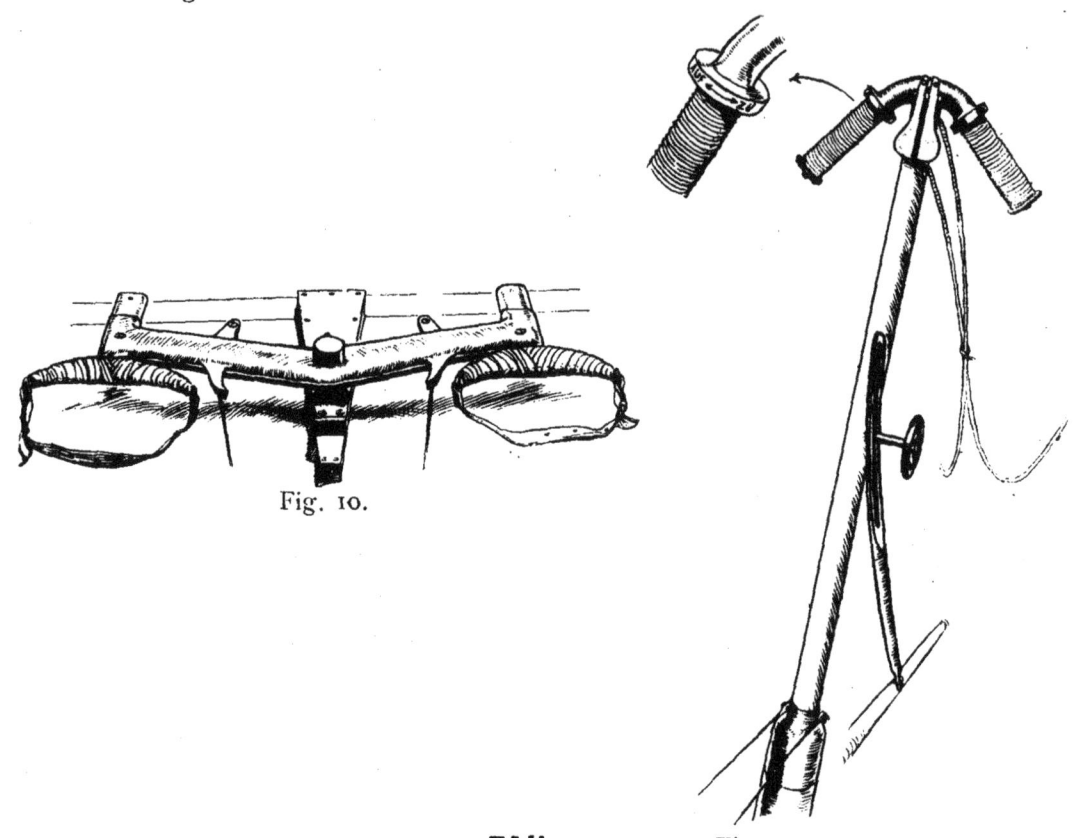

Fig. 10.

Fig. 11.

TAIL.

The fixed planes are noticed to have a flat top and a cambered lower surface, as in the Rumpler, although the camber is not so pronounced in the present machine.

The elevator is not divided, since the rudder is of such a shape as not to interfere with free elevator movement. The vertical fin has a wooden framework covered with three-ply, and is neatly faired off into the fuselage. The balanced rudder is of light welded steel framework, and is covered with fabric. The framework of both tail planes and elevators is of wood. (See Figs. 12, 14 and 15.)

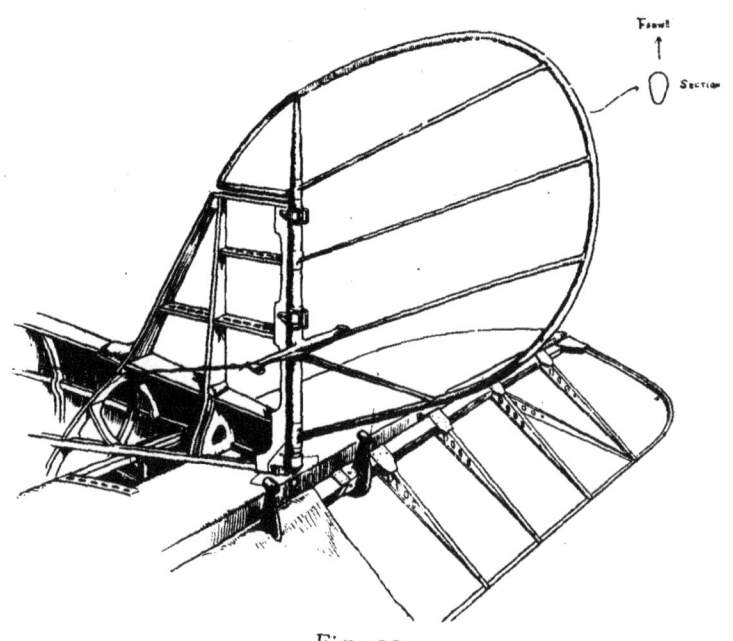

Fig. 12.

THE TAIL SKID.

Though of unusual design, the skid performs its functions satisfactorily, and is fixed in such a manner as not to be liable to weaken the sternpost. Its shape may be gathered from Fig. 13.

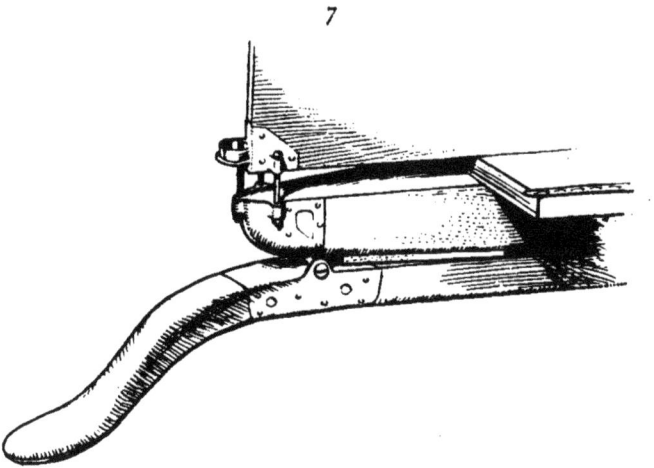

Fig. 13.

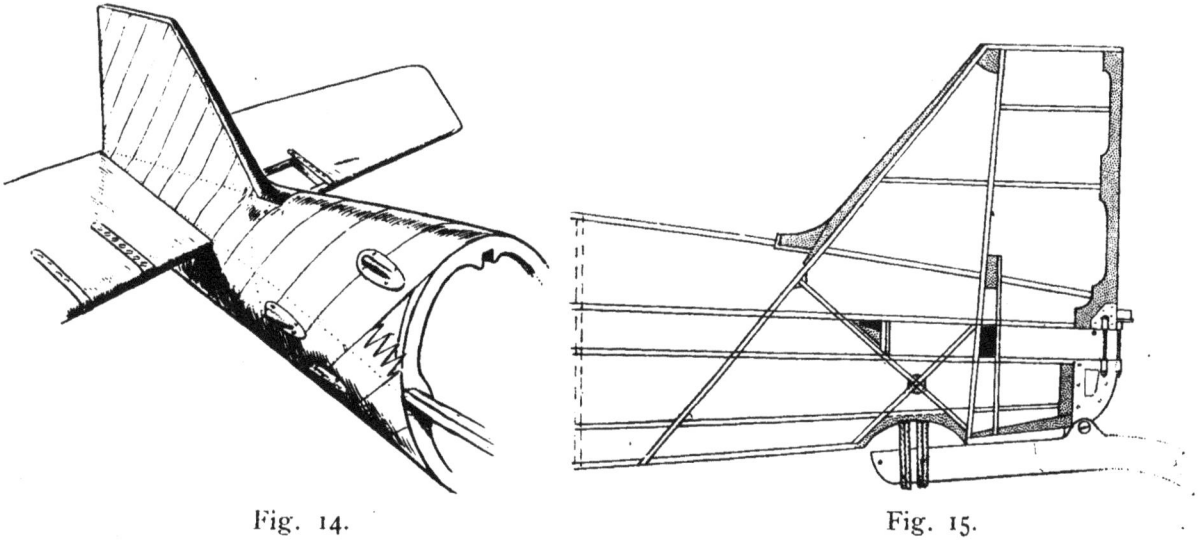

Fig. 14.   Fig. 15.

ENGINE.

The engine, a 160 H.P. Mercedes, No. 35482 BN 669 R.N. 83, guaranteed till 4/4/18, is mounted on wooden bearers, which are supported on transverse bulkheads of wood. The controls are very conveniently arranged. Besides the usual quadrant control, which is placed at the pilot's left hand, the port-side limb of the inverted vee, which forms the head of the control lever, is a twist grip throttle.

The quadrant control works in connection with the twist grip, and may also be used separately. Reference to Fig. 11 will make this clear.

PETROL SYSTEM.

The main petrol tank holds 12½ gallons, and is to be found in front of the pilot, underneath the ammunition magazines. It works, of course, under pressure, which is first supplied by the hand pump, and then maintained by the air pump driven by the engine camshaft.

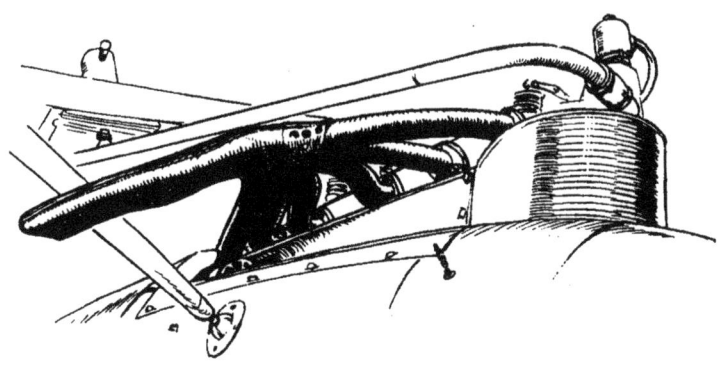

Fig. 16.

A secondary gravity tank capable of containing 9 gallons is situated in the port-side of the centre section, balancing the radiator. The filler-cap of this tank is visible in the photograph of the machine as seen from the rear.

The oil system is of the usual Mercedes type; the engine sump contains 2¾ gallons; and the small tank placed alongside the engine holds 1¼ gallons.

RADIATOR.

As is common German practice, the radiator (Fig. 17), is placed in the centre section, on the starboard side. The tubes are placed horizontally and are of oval section. Aluminium

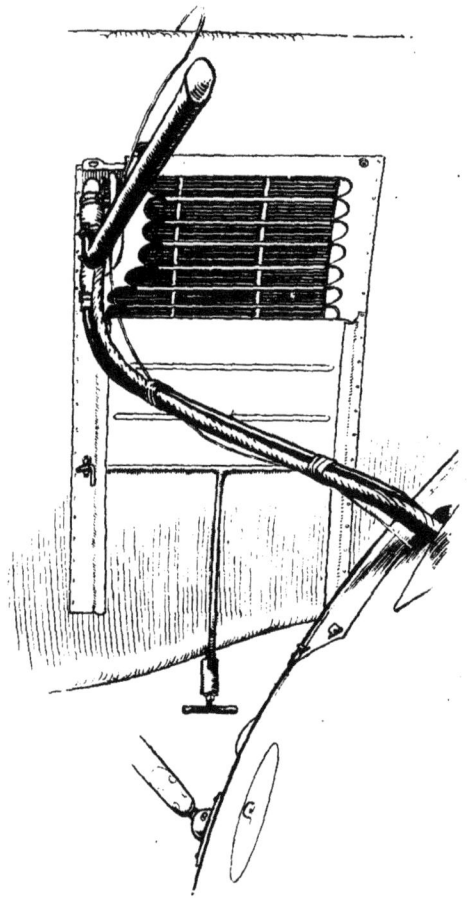

Fig 17.

deflecting fins are fixed on to the lower side, and a water head is maintained by means of a small vertical tank of stream-line cross section, to the top of which is fixed a small conical pipe with the wide end open and facing forward.

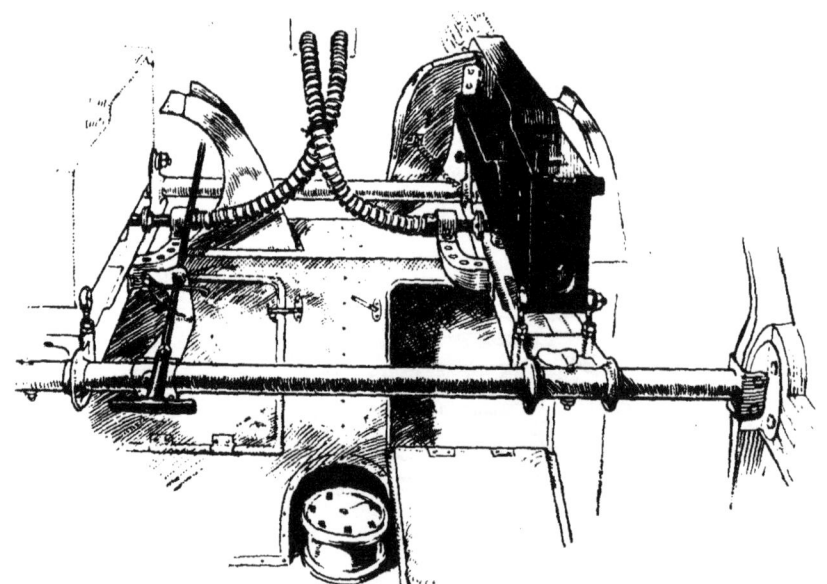

Fig. 18.

ARMAMENT.

The pilot controls the fire of two Spandau guns (Nos. 7961, 7602), arranged one on either side of the engine, inside the cowl. The triggers which operate the interrupter gear are in their usual place at the head of the control column.

The guns are not accessible during flight. (See Fig. 18.)

INSTRUMENTS.

These present no unusual features. There is no dashboard, the instruments being distributed in convenient positions in the cockpit. The compass is placed on the right hand side of pilot's seat, in a low position, and the deviation card is dated 2/11/17.

A Maximall petrol gauge is fitted in the centre of machine in front of the rudder bar, on the top of the main tank.

FABRIC AND DOPE.

The fabric appears to be flax; it is of the ordinary highly calendered type, but somewhat finer and thinner than the average.

Sections show that a fairly thick layer of clear dope had been followed by a thin layer of aluminium dope, very unevenly applied.

CAMOUFLAGE.

This machine is not camouflaged with the usual printed fabric, but presents a silvery appearance on account of the aluminium dope. The tail is painted a fairly dark brown, with the two colours meeting abruptly in a line.

PROPELLER.

This is an Axial No. 6334. diameter 2770; pitch 2200. There are seven laminations— one of walnut, three of mahogany, and three of sycamore.

This aeroplane is to be seen at the Enemy Aircraft View Rooms, Agricultural Hall, Islington. The necessary pass may be obtained by writing to The Controller, Technical Dept., (Ap.D.L.), Central House, Kingsway, W.C. 2.

W. G. A. Ap.D.(L.).

J. G. WEIR,
Brigadier-General,
Controller, Technical Department.

Front View.

Side View.

Rear View.

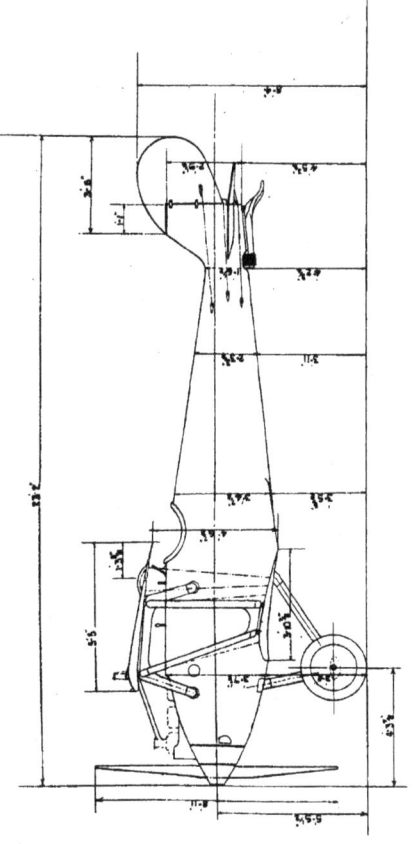

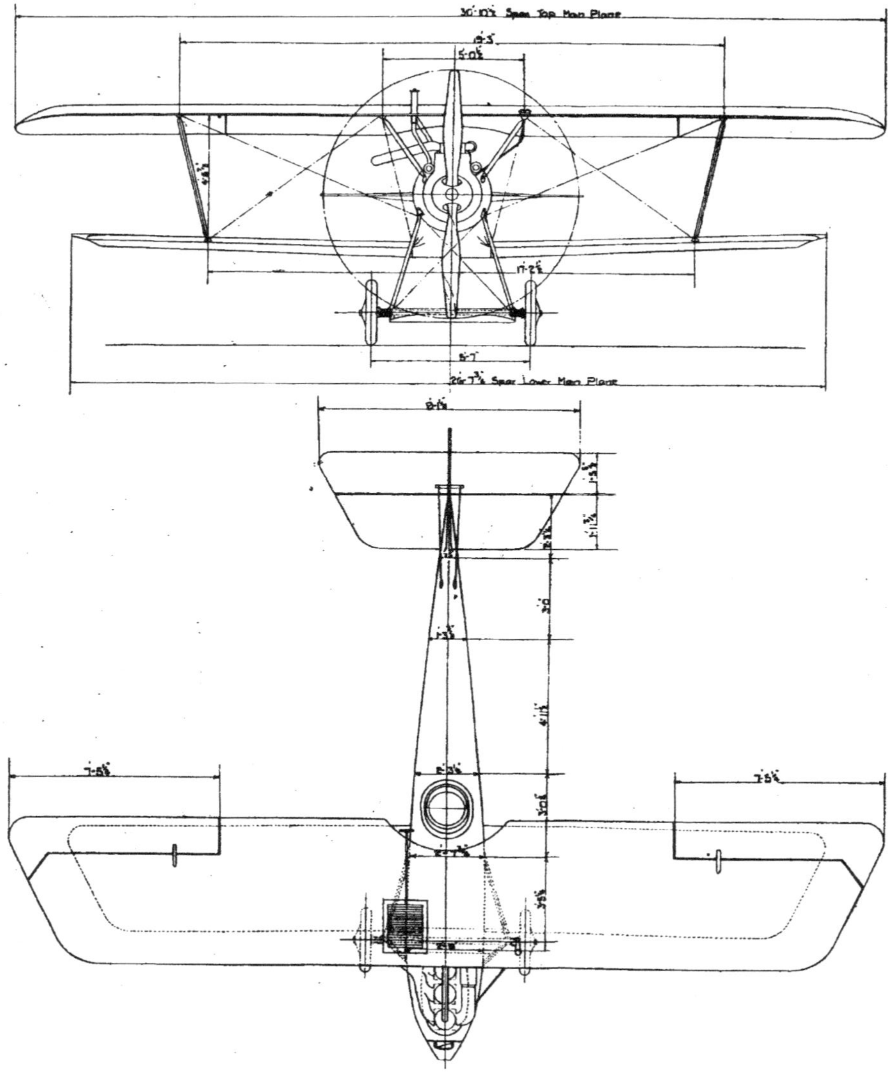

PFALZ SCOUT

SCALE A = ½, 1 FOOT

Span of Top Plane	30' 10¼"
Span of Lower Plane	26' 7¼"
Length Overall	23' 2"
Gap at Inner Struts	4' 9¼"
Gap at Outer Struts	4' 6¼"
Chord of Top Plane	5' 5¼"
Chord of Lower Plane	3' 11"
Angle of Incidence	6° 20'
Dihedral Angle (Lower Plane)	1°

www.ingramcontent.com/pod-product-compliance
Ingram Content Group UK Ltd.
Pitfield, Milton Keynes, MK11 3LW, UK
UKHW051526180426
11947UKWH00019B/1594